1001 DAD JOKES

Also available

1001 One-Liners
The Grumpy Old Gits' Joke Book
Old Age and How to Milk It

About the Author

Geoff Tibballs is the author of over 150 books, including the bestselling *Mammoth Book of Jokes*, *The Mammoth Book of Dirty Jokes*, *The Mammoth Book of Comic Quotes*, *The Seniors' Survival Guide* and *Dad-isms*. He has contributed to the *Ripley's Believe It or Not!* annuals for more than twenty years. He lives in Nottingham with his wife.

1001 DAD JOKES

SO BAD THEY'RE ALMOST GOOD!

G:

G:

Published in 2025
by Gemini Gift Books
Part of Gemini Books Group

Based in Woodbridge and London

Marine House, Tide Mill Way,
Woodbridge, Suffolk IP12 1AP
United Kingdom

www.geminibooks.com

Text © 2025 Gemini Gift Books Ltd
Design and layout © 2025 Gemini Gift Books Ltd
Typeset by Danny Lyle

ISBN 978-1-80247-269-1

A CIP catalogue record for this book is available from the British Library.

Manufacturer's EU Representative: Eurolink Compliance
Limited, 25 Herbert Place, Dublin, D02 AY86, Republic
of Ireland. admin@eurolink-europe.ie

Printed in the UK

10 9 8 7 6 5 4 3 2 1

FSC
www.fsc.org
MIX
Paper | Supporting
responsible forestry
FSC® C018072

Welcome to a treasure trove of golden gags

As well as trying to find a cure for the common cold, scientists are believed to be working hard in an attempt to identify the gene that makes dads think they're funny. Because, once men become parents, for some unknown reason they suddenly develop an unquenchable thirst for telling their children jokes so corny that many belong inside a Christmas cracker next to a paper hat. The dad joke is to classic humour what junk food is to haute cuisine. But all styles of humour have their merits and, despite their shortcomings, dad jokes have turned into something of an art form. They are so bad they're almost good. They have become as much a rite of fatherhood as changing nappies and rhythmless dancing at family weddings.

The classic dad joke is short, inoffensive and consists of a ridiculously contrived set-up followed by an excruciating pun which elicits a combination of pained groans and eye-rolls from his captive audience but unconfined joy from the teller himself. Although dad jokes are only really designed to amuse one person, they are told with such unashamed enthusiasm that occasionally – just occasionally – his children might find themselves having to suppress a snigger. It has to be said, however, that this is usually done more out of pity than genuine amusement.

Often cheesier than a four-cheese pizza and lamer than a three-legged horse, this collection of more than 1,001 dad jokes will have you rocking with laughter and your children threatening to disown you.

Don't say you haven't been warned.

"DAD, SHALL I PUT THE KETTLE ON?"

"OKAY. IF YOU THINK IT WILL SUIT YOU."

Why was the cowboy cautious when he came across a small tree with strips of smoked pork hanging from its branches?
He was worried it might be a hambush.

Why is Shrek such a good gardener?
Because he's got green fingers.

Did you see that someone stole all the toilets from the local police station? The police say they have nothing to go on.

What do you get when you drop a piano down a mine shaft?
A flat miner.

Why did the two boa constrictors get married?
Because they had a crush on each other.

Did you read that one of the Russian acrobats in a circus human pyramid has been deported?
Now the others don't have Oleg to stand on.

Why did all the young military cadets faint as soon as the general began inspecting them?
They had been told it was a passing out parade.

What's round, and has a circumference, a radius, a diameter and a sharp set of teeth?
A vicious circle.

Did you read about the woman who suddenly noticed that she had a small picnic table and benches growing on the side of her face?
The doctor told her not to worry, it's only a beauty spot.

What was the name of that boy in your class whose car was stolen from the school car park?
Oh yes, I remember – Carlos.

My dad wanted me to become a fruit farmer like him, but I said I was too scared to do it.
So he told me to grow a pear.

Did you hear about the skydiver who quit his job?
He fell out with his boss.

"DAD, HOW DID YOU MANAGE TO EAT SUCH A BIG SLICE OF CHOCOLATE GÂTEAU?"

"IT WAS NOTHING. IT WAS A PIECE OF CAKE."

How is a pig's tail like someone who arrives at the airport five hours before their flight is due to depart?
Both are twirly.

What did the buffalo say to his son when he dropped him off at school?
Bison.

Did you read about the man who started a *cold*-air balloon business?
It never got off the ground.

Why shouldn't you trust atoms?
Because they make up everything.

Why did the woman take a pencil and a thin sheet of paper to the police station?
Because she wanted detectives to trace someone.

What is sweet, sugary, very hairy and swings through the trees of Borneo?
A meringue utan.

The man who stole my diary just died.
My thoughts are with his family.

Did you read about the man who has a deep-rooted phobia about German sausages?
Apparently he always fears the wurst.

Where did the cat go when it lost its tail?
To the retail store.

What lives in Zurich, can cut wires, open cans and bottles, put in screws, saw through wood, clean horses' hooves, cook delicious meals and be a loving partner?
A Swiss Army wife.

I bought a thesaurus last week, but when I got home and opened it, all the pages were blank.
There are no words to describe how angry I was.

"DAD, CAN YOU CALL ME A TAXI."

"YOU'RE A TAXI."

What do you get if you cross a frisbee with a cow?
Skimmed milk.

Why did the farmer plough his field with a steam roller?
Because he wanted to grow mashed potatoes.

5

Did you hear about the English tourist in Rome who went to see the Spanish Steps?
He was disappointed to discover they weren't a tribute band.

Shortly after his death, why could Mozart's symphonies be heard playing in reverse from his grave?
He was decomposing.

What's the difference between unlawful and illegal?
One is something that is against the law and the other is a sick bird of prey.

"DAD, ARE YOU GOING TO PUT THE CHRISTMAS TREE UP YOURSELF?"

"NO, I THINK IT WOULD LOOK BETTER IN THE HALLWAY."

What makes the Leaning Tower of Pisa lean?
It doesn't eat much.

Why did the man quit his job as a can crusher?
Because it was soda pressing.

How do monkeys fly from jungle to jungle?
By hot air baboon.

I just can't get enough of old Spanish architecture.
It's so Moorish.

Why don't owls go on dates when it's raining?
Because it's too wet to woo.

Did you read about the man who opened an origami business?
It folded.

Cosmetic surgery used to be such a taboo subject.
But now you can talk about Botox and nobody raises an eyebrow.

My wife likes me to blow on her whenever she gets too warm.
But, to be honest, I'm not a fan.

Did you hear about the recent online survey?

It showed that six out of seven dwarfs aren't Happy.

What's brown, stinks and sounds like a bell?
Dung.

What was the name of that boy in your class who had three eyes?
Oh yes, I remember – Seymour.

What do you get if you cross a vampire and a circus entertainer?
Something who goes straight for the juggler.

I went on an adventure weekend where I had to wear a colourful bird costume, leap from a high bridge and dangle on an elastic rope suspended above the ground.
It was weird. I don't think I'll be going budgie jumping again.

Did you know that bees are capable of sneezing? In fact, if you were to ask me what is my favourite garden sound, that would be it.
It's the bee sneeze.

"DAD, WHAT DID YOU WATCH LAST NIGHT AFTER WE'D GONE TO BED?"

"MUM AND I WATCHED TWO DVDS BACK TO BACK. LUCKILY I WAS THE ONE FACING THE TV."

What do you call a pig that has lost its voice?
Disgruntled.

What did the slice of bread say to the slice of cheese?
'You're the best thing since me.'

Did you read that the ice-cream parlour in town has been forced to close down and the owner has had to sell all the equipment to businesses in the area?
The local newspaper got the scoop.

My boss said he is going to fire someone in the company for having bad posture.
I have a hunch it could be me.

Did you read about the man who repeatedly broke wind in the elevator of a multi-storey car park?
It was wrong on so many levels.

What award does the Dentist of the Year receive?
A little plaque.

Your grandfather warned people that *Titanic* would sink.
No one listened, but he kept on and on warning them until eventually they got sick of him and threw him out of the cinema.

How did the picture end up in jail?
It was framed.

What was the name of that girl in your class who had one leg shorter than the other?
Oh yes, I remember – Eileen.

What do you call a can-opener that doesn't work?
A can't-opener.

Did you read about the man who was convinced that he was a pair of curtains?
The doctor told him to pull himself together.

What has four legs, doe eyes, horns and a tail, roams the African savannah, and tortures and butchers people?
Vlad the Impala.

What do you call a baptism where everyone is in fancy dress?
A blessing in disguise.

How do you turn a duck into a soul singer?
Put it in the microwave until its bill withers.

"DAD, CAN YOU PUT MY SHOES ON?"

"I DON'T THINK THEY'LL FIT ME."

I just got home after a disastrous weekend break on Humberside.
Yes, I've been to Hull and back.

Did you hear that the police are looking for a man with one eye?
If they don't find him, they're going to use both eyes.

Why do golfers take an extra pair of socks when they set off to play a round?
In case they get a hole in one.

Why shouldn't you be afraid of baby aardvarks?
Because, as the saying goes, a little aardvark never hurt anyone.

Did you read about the rookie police officer who put a set of handcuffs on the door of a two-storey building?
He was making a house arrest.

People say they pick their nose, but I feel like I was just born with mine.

What do you get if you fill a cake with chocolate, cream, fruit and a stick of dynamite?
A gâteau blaster.

To promote ecology, our cases were carried to our hotel room by a porter dressed as a bluebottle.
But I didn't reward him, because fly-tipping is illegal.

Who was the roundest knight at King Arthur's Round Table?
Sir Cumference.

What did the plumber say when he decided to break up with his girlfriend, Florence?
"It's all over, Flo."

Did you read that a pencil which was once owned by William Shakespeare went up for auction last week?
The only problem is that it had been badly chewed, so they can't tell whether it's 2B or not 2B.

When Tonto was short of money, who did he turn to for help?
The Loan Arranger.

To the person who stole my bed, I won't rest until I find you.

Why did the bicycle fall over?
It was two tired.

"DAD, DO YOU KNOW HOW TO MAKE AN APPLE TURNOVER?"

"YES, IT'S EASY. YOU PUSH IT DOWN A HILL."

Have you heard about these new corduroy pillowcases?
I'd be surprised if you haven't because they've been making lots of headlines.

What was the name of that boy in your class who got into serious debt?
Oh yes, I remember – Owen.

Did you read about the taxi driver who lost his job for always going the extra mile?

I bought a nice slice of tongue for my lunch, but, while my back was turned, the cat got it.
I was speechless.

Why was Cinderella such a terrible figure skater?
Because her coach was a pumpkin.

Did you see that a police officer caught two kids playing with a car battery and a firework?
He charged one and let the other one off.

For years I have experienced an obsessive, over-whelming determination to collect every Beatles album.
I need Help!

What do you get if you put a duck in a cement mixer?
Quacks in the pavement.

Did you read about the man who ate small metal wire clips every day?
In fact, it was his staple diet.

If you want to get on in life, why should you not waste your time collecting postage stamps?
Because philately will get you nowhere.

Why was the slice of bread sent home from school?
Because it was feeling crummy.

I tried drag racing for the first time last week, but it's really difficult trying to run in a short skirt and heels.

"LOOK, DAD! A FLOCK OF COWS."

"NOT A FLOCK. A HERD."

"HERD OF COWS?"

"OF COURSE I'VE HEARD OF COWS! THERE ARE SOME IN THAT FIELD."

Did you read the sad story about the unemployed contortionist?
He says he can no longer make ends meet.

Why did the pharmacist walk around on tiptoe?
She didn't want to wake the sleeping pills.

How did the house feel after its entire interior was destroyed by fire?
It was gutted.

Did you hear about the shepherd who drove his sheep through town?
He was arrested for making a ewe turn.

What is as big as an elephant but weighs nothing?
Its shadow.

I recently bumped into the man who sold me a miniature antique globe.
It's a small world.

Where does a farmer find new cows to buy?
In a cattlelog.

Did you read about the man who was convinced he was a horse? He used to trot, neigh and canter like a horse but was eventually admitted to hospital after eating nothing but hay for a month.
His condition is said to be stable.

Why do sopranos make good sailors?
Because they love to hit the high Cs.

What did Frida, the magician, say to the audience after making her assistant, Hans, disappear?
"Look! No Hans."

I'm sceptical of anyone who tells me they do yoga every day.
To me, it's a bit of a stretch.

"DAD, DO THEY SERVE MUSSELS IN THIS RESTAURANT?"

"THEY'LL SERVE ANYONE."

What's bad-tempered and goes with custard?
Apple grumble.

Did you read about the plumber who quit his job because his company was going down the drain?

Do you know the last thing my father said to me before he kicked the bucket?
"Son, watch how far I can kick this bucket."

Did you hear about the boy who drowned in a bowl of muesli?
A strong currant pulled him under.

What do you call a donkey with only three legs?
A wonkey.

What was the name of that boy in your class who came in one day with a really severe haircut?
Oh yes, I remember – Shaun.

What do you call a short-sighted dinosaur?
D'youthink'esaurus.

Did you read about the girl who always wanted to be a hula dancer? It wasn't easy for her.
To achieve her ambition she had to jump through a lot of hoops.

Have you ever read about the medieval monarch who was only 12 inches tall?
Apparently he was a terrible king, but he made a great ruler.

How did the barber win the marathon?
He knew a short cut.

I went to the doctor with a suspicious-looking mole.
She said they all look that way and I should have left him in the garden.

"DAD, MY BEDROOM IS ALWAYS SO COLD."

"WHY DON'T YOU STAND IN THE CORNER? IT'S ALWAYS 90 DEGREES THERE."

Did you read about the two TV aerials that got married?
Apparently the wedding ceremony was lousy, but the reception was great.

What did the chick say when the mother hen laid an orange instead of an egg?
"Look at the orange mama laid."

What was the name of that girl in your class whose shoe fell apart at the school prom?
Oh yes, I remember – Lucille.

Did you hear the rumour about butter?
Well, I'm not going to spread it.

Why did the banana go to the doctor?
Because it wasn't peeling very well.

What do you get if you feed a whole roast duck to a hungry cat?
A duck-filled fatty puss.

Did you hear what happened at the world's shortest game of tag?
It was touch and go for a second.

What is the only cheese that is made backwards?
Edam.

What did the Russian revolutionary say when he knocked on the door of the Imperial Palace in 1917?
"Is Len in?"

What do you call a snowman in June?
A puddle.

Did I ever tell you about the time that my father finished runner-up in a county golf tournament to Sister Margaret from St Agnes's Convent?
Wonderful man. Second to nun.

"DAD, WHY DON'T YOU EVER CRY WHEN YOU CHOP ONIONS?"

"WELL, SON, THE SECRET IS NOT TO GET TOO EMOTIONALLY ATTACHED TO THEM."

Your mother and I laugh about how competitive we are.
But I laugh more.

Did you read that someone smashed a large hole into the wall surrounding a nudist colony?
The police are looking into it.

My therapist told me I have trouble expressing my emotions.
I can't say I'm surprised.

Did you hear about the man who used to be a gravedigger?
He was sacked because one day he completely lost the plot.

Which is faster, hot or cold?
Hot, because you can catch a cold.

How do you get five donkeys on a fire engine?
Two in the front, two in the back, and one on the roof going, "Ee-aw-ee-aw-ee-aw..."

Which highly trained military fighter lives on a diet of fish and can balance a ball on the end of its nose?
A US Navy SEAL.

Why was the mushroom always invited to parties?
Because he was a fun guy.

Did you read about the problems on the set of *Frozen*?
Apparently Princess Elsa made a complaint about one of the other cast members and wouldn't let it go.

Last week, I accidentally swallowed a bottle of food colouring.
The doctor says I'm okay, but I feel like I've dyed a little inside.

"WHEN I'M AT THE SHOP, DO YOU WANT ME TO GET YOU A HAMAFER?"

"WHAT'S A HAMAFER, DAD?"

"KNOCKING NAILS IN."

What do a tick and the Eiffel Tower have in common?
They're both Paris sites.

What do you get if you cross a philosopher with a Mafia hitman?
Someone who will make you an offer you can't understand.

What do you call a line of people waiting to get their hair cut?
A barber queue.

Did you read about the new reality TV show that is looking to find the best Cher doppelganger?
It's called Cher and Cher Alike.

I took my dog to the vet this afternoon. I handed my dog to him and after he had quickly examined him the vet said, "I'm going to have to put your dog down."
I was shocked.
I said, "Why?"
The vet said, "Because he's heavy."

Did you read about the cartoonist who was found dead at his home?
Details are sketchy.

What was the name of that boy in your class who used to lie down at the front door of his house?

Oh yes, I remember – Matt.

What did the farmer say when he learned that his prized pedigree nanny goat was still not pregnant?
"You must be kidding!"

What happened to the boy who lost part of his video-game equipment?
He was inconsolable.

Did you read about the man who went on a tandem parachute jump?
Everything was going well until he fell off the bike.

What's made of leather and sounds like a sneeze?
A shoe.

Have you seen the YouTube video featuring the man with the worst cold ever?
It's gone viral.

My wife said I should do lunges to get in shape.
That would be a big step forward.

How can health experts be right when they say smoking is bad for you?
After all, it cures salmon.

"WHAT WAS THE RESTAURANT LIKE, DAD? HOW DID YOU FIND YOUR MEAL?"

"I JUST LOOKED ON THE PLATE AND THERE IT WAS!"

Did you read that a new dating service has opened in Prague?
It's called Czech Mate.

Why didn't the skeleton go to the high school prom?
Because it had no body to go with.

What do you get if you cross a skunk with a hot-air balloon?
Something that stinks to high heaven.

I start a new job in Seoul next week.
I hope it's going to be a good Korea move.

What did the surgeon say to the patient who insisted on doing his own stitches?
"Suture self."

Did you know that hundreds of years ago scientists divided the week up into seven 24-hour periods? They tried to think of a snappier name for each of these periods, but eventually became bored with the whole process.
So they decided to call it a day.

Why do hummingbirds hum?
Because they can't remember the words.

Instead of playing gentle music, my new bedside alarm clock shouts a stream of insults.
I think I'm in for a rude awakening.

What do you call a fish with no eyes?
A fsh.

Did you read about the inventor who spent years developing the idea of a pencil with a rubber at both ends before eventually realizing it was pointless?

Why did the man always wear a helmet when he sat down to dinner?
He was on a crash diet.

My doctor told me that jogging could add years to my life.
He was right – I feel ten years older already.

"DAD, I CAN'T ANSWER THE DOOR IN MY PYJAMAS."

"WHY HAVE YOU GOT A DOOR IN YOUR PYJAMAS?"

Did you read about the pizza delivery guy who was found dead with his body covered in pepperoni, olives, mushrooms, onion, slices of ham and spicy beef?
The police think he topped himself.

Why did the old man fall down the well?
Because he couldn't see that well.

What was the name of that boy in your class who had delusions that he lived in a casserole dish?
Oh yes, I remember – Stu.

My advice is, never trust stairs.
They're always up to something.

Did you see that the man who designs cul-de-sacs has decided to quit?
He said it was a dead-end job.

Why did the tortoise go to assertiveness classes?
To try and bring him out of his shell.

I keep a cute amphibian as a pet.
I call him Tiny because he's my newt.

What do you get if a herd of elephants tramples Batman and Robin?
Flatman and Ribbon.

Do you know why the divorce rate among tennis players is so high?
Because love means nothing to them.

When my wife told me that I should stop impersonating a flamingo, I had to put my foot down.

I asked the supermarket assistant where I could find the Arnold Schwarzenegger vitamin packs.
He said, "Aisle B, back."

Did you hear about the man who walked into a bar ... and immediately lost the limbo contest?

My doctor has strongly advised me to stop playing the drums.
He lives in the flat below.

"DAD, I'M OFF."

"I THOUGHT THERE WAS A STRANGE SMELL."

Did you read about the man who fell into an upholstery machine?
Happily, he is fully recovered.

Why should you never lie to an X-ray technician?
Because they can see right through you.

What do you get if you watch a Jackie Chan movie backwards?
A movie about a guy who can assemble furniture with his feet.

What did the alpaca say to his date?
"Do you want to go on a picnic? Alpaca lunch."

Did you read about the giant who suffered a terrible bout of diarrhoea?
No? I'm surprised. It's all over town.

Why was the cannibal ill after eating his ex-wife?
Because he had eaten something that didn't agree with him.

After going out together for a week, why did the physicist and the biologist break up?
Because they had no chemistry.

I can't stand stair lifts.
They drive me up the wall.

What happens to an illegally parked frog?
It gets toad away.

Did you read about the woman who asked her husband to pass her the lipstick, but he accidentally gave her the glue stick instead?
She still isn't talking to him.

What was the name of that girl in your class who had just a single tooth in her mouth?
Oh yes, I remember – Juanita.

Why was King Charles told he was being pedantic by keeping Prince William and Prince Harry apart?
Because he was just splitting heirs.

What do you call cattle with a sense of humour?
Laughing stock.

My grandfather's motto was: "Always fight fire with fire."
It was also why he was sacked from his job with the fire service.

Did you hear what happened to the man who worked at the computer keyboard factory?
He got fired for not putting in enough shifts.

"DAD, YOU'RE A LOUSY DRIVER."

"WHAT DO YOU MEAN? ONLY THE OTHER DAY SOMEONE COMPLIMENTED ME ON MY PARKING. THEY LEFT A NOTE ON MY WINDSHIELD THAT SAID 'PARKING FINE'."

How do you know if an elephant is sitting behind you in the bathtub?
You can smell the peanuts on his breath.

I never like to go to funerals if they start before noon.
I guess I'm simply not a mourning person.

What did the doctor say to the patient who had a strawberry growing out of his ear?
"Put come cream on it."

I couldn't believe that my dad had been stealing from his job as a road worker.
But when I got home all the signs were there.

What do you call a *Star Wars* droid that goes the long way round?
R2 Detour.

Did you see that the police want to interview a man wearing high heels and lace knickers?
But the Chief Constable said they must wear their normal uniforms.

Why was the national park ranger pleased to see that all the wildebeest had left the game reserve?
Because no gnus is good news.

How do bakers exchange recipes with one another?
Strictly on a knead-to-know basis.

Did you read about the cowboy who opened a German car dealership in Wyoming just so that he could be an Audi partner?

My wife dated a clown before she went out with me.
I don't mind admitting I had some pretty big shoes to fill.

> "DAD, HAVE YOU HAD A HAIRCUT?"

> "NO, I GOT THEM ALL CUT."

Did you hear about the man who broke his arm in two places?
The doctor told him to stop going to those places.

What was the name of that girl in your class who used to hear through an electronic keyboard that had been surgically grafted to the side of her head?
Oh yes, I remember – Cynthia.

Let me tell you about your grandfather. He was a good man, a brave man.
He had the heart of a lion and a lifetime ban from the zoo.

Why did Captain Kirk go into the ladies' toilet?
To boldly go where no man has gone before.

Did you read about the man who drove his car into church last Sunday morning?
He said he wanted to take it for a service.

I've been to the dentist on numerous occasions, so it's fair to say I know the drill.

Why was the belt arrested?
For holding up a pair of jeans.

When the insects played the invertebrates at football, why did the millipede miss the kick-off?
Because he was still putting on his boots.

Did you hear about the man who was fired from his job marking exam papers?
He couldn't understand it. He always gave 110 per cent.

What jewellery should you wear if you have no neck?
A neckless.

What was the name of that girl in your class who was an expert on things you'd find in a budgie's cage?
Oh yes, I remember – Mirabelle.

"DAD, A POLICE OFFICER IS AT THE DOOR. HE SAYS OUR DOG HAS BEEN CHASING SOMEONE ON A BIKE."

"TELL HIM IT'S NONSENSE. OUR DOG DOESN'T EVEN OWN A BIKE."

A furniture store has been calling and texting me every day for over a week. It's driving me crazy. They just won't let it go.
All I wanted was one night stand.

What do you get from a pampered cow?
Spoiled milk.

What's yellow, fruity and mean?
A banana with a grudge.

Have you watched that new film about fly-fishing?
I hear it has an impressive cast.

A man called at the house the other day offering special rates on burial plots.
I thought, "That's the last thing I need."

I told your mother she was drawing her eyebrows too high.
She looked surprised.

Did you read about the man who has started to invest in stocks – beef, chicken and vegetable?
One day he hopes to be a bouillonaire.

What did the drummer call his twin daughters?
Anna One, Anna Two...

I asked the doctor whether the cream he was prescribing would definitely clear up my red, pimply skin.
But he said he never made rash promises.

Did you read about the woman who stole from a shop while balancing on the shoulders of a trio of vampires?
She was charged with shoplifting on three counts.

"DAD, WHAT ARE YOU BUYING MUM FOR HER BIRTHDAY?"

"I'M THINKING ABOUT GETTING HER A NEW FRIDGE SO I CAN WATCH HER FACE LIGHT UP WHEN SHE OPENS IT."

What do you get if you cross a pig with a telephone?
A lot of crackling on the line.

What do you call an overweight monk who meditates?
A deep-fat friar.

Why do you often see lambs going into betting shops?
Because they love to gambol.

Lance is an uncommon name nowadays, but in medieval times people were named Lance a lot.

Did you read about the man who used to be addicted to soap?
It's okay. He's clean now.

Why are basketball courts always wet?
Because the players dribble so much.

Did you read about the fisherman who tried to claim on his insurance after a shoal of fish badly damaged his net?
The insurance company refused to pay up because they said it was an act of cod.

What's purple, round and cries for help from a fruit tree?
A damson in distress.

What was the name of that girl in your class who was always complaining about things?
Oh yes, I remember – Mona.

In which hospital department do patients spend the day sitting around solemnly reciting Scottish poetry?
The Serious Burns Unit.

Which is the most generous vegetable?
The artichoke. It has a big heart.

Did you read that the former egg chef at the Ritz now has the world's largest *Super Mario* collection?
It sounds like a classic case of poacher turned gamekeeper.

I've been thinking about taking up meditation.
I figure it's better than sitting around all day doing nothing.

Did you read about the man who was kidnapped by a gang of mime artists?
They did unspeakable things to him.

What do you call people who are afraid of Father Christmas?
Santa Claustrophobic.

Did you know that a slice of apple pie is £2.50 in Jamaica, £2.75 in Antigua and £3 in the Bahamas?
It's true. They are the pie rates of the Caribbean.

Why did the man decide to sell his vacuum cleaner?
Because all it was doing was gathering dust.

"DAD, WHAT SHOULD I PUT ON MY JOB APPLICATION FORM? THEY WANT TO KNOW IF I CAN PERFORM UNDER PRESSURE."

"PUT 'I'M NOT SURE BUT I CAN HAVE A GOOD CRACK AT "BOHEMIAN RHAPSODY"'."

What was the name of that boy in your class who, in all his years at the school, never did anything unexpected?

Oh yes, I remember – Norm.

My young son said I had ruined his birthday. I told him that was nonsense.

I didn't even know it was his birthday.

Why do seagulls fly over the sea?
Because if they flew over the bay, they would be bagels.

Did you hear about the man who quit his job in a shoe-recycling depot because it was sole-destroying?

Why did the accountant put all of his client's files and invoices in the oven?
He was trying to cook the books.

To the person who stole my glasses, I will find you.
I have contacts.

What's orange and sounds like a parrot?
A carrot.

"DAD, WILL YOU MAKE ME A SANDWICH?"

"ABRACADABRA! YOU'RE A SANDWICH."

Have you seen the new movie called *Constipated*?
Oh no, I forgot, it hasn't come out yet.

Did you read about the man who sadly passed away because he couldn't remember his blood type?
Apparently his final words to his family were, "Be positive."

When I arrived at the restaurant, the chef rudely announced that he was refusing to cook any salty or spicy dishes that evening.
It was all most unsavoury.

Why did the fugitive who was on the run from the police cut off the legs of his bed?
He wanted to lie low for a while.

What did one hat say to the other hat?
"You stay here, I'll go on ahead."

I called a gym instructor because I wanted him to teach me to do the splits. He asked me how flexible I was.
I told him I couldn't do Tuesdays.

Why did the secret agent wear a jacket covered in leaves and twigs?
He was working for Special Branch.

What type of films do hens like best?
Chick flicks.

Did you read that someone has opened a new restaurant on the moon?
Apparently the food is great but there's no atmosphere.

Why did Sherlock Holmes's house have a yellow front door?
It was a lemon entry, my dear Watson.

Did you hear about the lobster that got a job at Pizza Hut?
He works at the crust station.

My doctor advised me to take supplements.
I thought I'd start with the Telegraph *and work my way up to the* Sunday Times.

Why aren't dogs good dancers?
Because they've got two left feet.

Did you hear about the confused man who sat up all night wondering where the sun had gone?
The next morning it dawned on him.

"DAD, CAN YOU GIVE ME A LIFT?"

"SURE. YOU'RE TALENTED, CLEVER AND BEAUTIFUL."

What's the difference between an injured lion and a wet day?
One roars with pain and the other pours with rain.

What was the name of that boy in your class who used to bite other boys and suck their blood?
Oh yes, I remember – Nat.

Did you hear about the man who woke up suddenly to find a horse lying next to him in bed?
It was a night mare.

Why was the sailor found balancing awkwardly on one leg on top of a pack of playing cards?
Because his commander told him to stand on the deck.

What's the best way to watch a fly-fishing tournament?
Livestream.

A priest, a minister and a rabbit walk into a bar.
The rabbit says, "I think I might be a typo."

Did you hear about the circus ringmaster who spent all day just hanging around his workplace doing nothing?
He was charged with loitering within tent.

Which member of the deer family would you expect to find in a hair salon?
The styling moose.

What do you call a snowman with a six-pack?
An abdominal snowman.

Did you know that the girl who lives at number 15 walked out on her boyfriend after discovering that he has only nine toes?
It turns out that she's lack toes intolerant.

Did you read about the man who named his dogs Rolex and Timex because he wanted watchdogs?

"DAD, WHY DO YOU AND MUM NEVER ARGUE?"

"AS A MATTER OF FACT, WE HAD A MINOR DISAGREEMENT LAST NIGHT. WE WERE ARGUING ABOUT WHOSE TURN IT WAS TO LOAD UP THE WASHING MACHINE. EVENTUALLY I THREW IN THE TOWEL."

My wife realized I was cheating on her when she found all the letters I had been hiding. She was so angry she said she's never playing Scrabble with me again.

What's the difference between a cat and a comma?
One has claws at the end of its paws, the other is a pause at the end of a clause.

Why can't leopards hide?
Because they're always spotted.

What was the name of that boy in your class who had a rubber toe?
Oh yes, I remember – Roberto.

Why are elephants wrinkled?
Have you ever tried to iron one?

Did you hear what happened to the ATM that became addicted to money?
It suffered from withdrawals.

Where do people with nasty rashes go to meet other people with nasty rashes?
A shingles bar.

Why does everyone in the USA own a tank top?
Because they have the right to bare arms.

What did the botanist get when he crossed a dahlia with a fuchsia?
A failure, because it didn't have much of a fuchsia.

Did you hear about the man who walked into a bar with a piece of asphalt under his arm and said, "A beer, please, and one for the road."

I'm writing a book that will eventually be about hurricanes and tornados.
It's only a draft at the moment.

"DAD, DON'T YOU THINK IT'S MUGGY TODAY?"

"NO, I THOUGHT IT WAS TUESDAY TODAY."

Did you hear about the man whose lifelong ambition was to be run over by a steam train?

When it finally happened he was chuffed to bits.

My wife likes to wear a necklace of beads.
It means I know I can always count on her.

Did you hear about the cross-eyed teacher?
She couldn't control her pupils.

And did you hear about the cross-eyed optician?
He could never see eye to eye with his patients.

Last week I went to the library and borrowed a book about sandpaper.
I found it in the friction section.

What did the zebra say the first time he saw a piano?
"Dad?"

How does Good King Wenceslas like his pizzas?
Deep pan, crisp and even.

Why did the shareholders of a compass-manufacturing company call an emergency meeting?
They were worried that the company wasn't heading in the right direction.

Where does a fish go to borrow money?
A loan shark.

Did you hear about the racing snail that decided to get rid of his shell?
He thought it would make him faster, but instead it just made him sluggish.

If you're thinking about working in a prison library, you'll need to consider both the prose and the cons.

"I HAD BAD DREAMS LAST NIGHT BECAUSE I ATE TOO MUCH LIQUORICE BEFORE I WENT TO BED."

"WHAT DID YOU DREAM ABOUT, DAD?"

"ALL SORTS."

Why was Cinderella never picked for the football team?
Because she kept running away from the ball.

I just bought the latest, state-of-the-art, solar-powered kitchen knife.
It's real cutting-edge technology.

Did you read about the woman who went to the capital of France, drank too much, fell from her hotel window and ended up in hospital in a body cast?
She vowed never again to get plastered in Paris.

What's the difference between a bowl of mouldy lettuce and a slow, depressing song?
One is a bad salad, and the other is a sad ballad.

What do you call a pig with no clothes on?
Streaky bacon.

A work colleague said, "Don't you think it's strange that you have a habit of leaning over towards me whenever you accept my point of view?"
I'm inclined to agree with him.

Why didn't the two melons run away to get married?
Because they cantaloupe.

Did you see that the man who invented the throat lozenge died last week?
There was no coffin at his funeral.

Mules can be used for carrying supplies and elephants are used for transporting logs, but what might you use a wombat for?
Playing wom.

What do you call someone who never breaks wind in public?
A private tutor.

I'm having difficulty keeping my hands warm with fingerless gloves.
Any tips?

What do you call a chicken that crosses the road, rolls in the mud and then crosses back again?
A dirty double-crosser.

That storm last night was terrible. A bolt of lightning landed in the toilet of a house along the road, but meteorologists say it probably won't happen again – it was just a flash in the pan.

I said to my eldest daughter, "If your latest boyfriend can't appreciate your fruit jokes, you need to let that mango."

"DAD, WHAT DO YOU REMEMBER ABOUT YOUR WEDDING DAY?"

"I REMEMBER IT BEING A VERY HAPPY AND EMOTIONAL OCCASION. EVEN THE CAKE WAS IN TIERS."

Why should you never use "beef stew" as an online password?
It's not stroganoff.

Did you see that the country's most distinguished door designer has quit his job?
He says he's looking for a new opening.

Why did the family dog have such a bad attitude?
Because he had a microchip on his shoulder.

What do Alexander the Great and Winnie the Pooh have in common?
They have the same middle name.

It's not that I don't know how to juggle, it's just that I don't have the balls to do it.

What did the full glass say to the empty glass?
"You look drunk."

Did you read about the theatre actor who alarmed the audience by falling down a gap in the floorboards?
It was just a stage he was going through.

I recently got a stepladder.
Sadly, I never knew my real ladder.

"DAD, DID YOU SEE THE MAN ACROSS THE ROAD WASHING THE CAR WITH HIS SON?"

"WHY DOESN'T HE USE A SPONGE LIKE EVERYONE ELSE?"

What was the name of that girl in your class who had teeth like a beaver?
Oh yes, I remember – Nora.

Why did the plain peanut hire a bodyguard?
It didn't want to be assaulted.

Did you hear about the stage assistant who asked the escapologist for a pay rise?
He told her he wanted to help but his hands were tied.

When my doctor told me that orthopaedic shoes would cure my back pain, I didn't believe him.
But I stand corrected.

What did the jar of mayonnaise say when somebody opened the door of the fridge?
"Hey, close the door. I'm dressing!"

I took a poll the other day.
And it turns out that 100 per cent of the people inside the tent were angry when it collapsed.

What did the boy say to his sister when he saw her crying?
"Are you having a crisis?"

Apparently the devil is losing his hair.
They reckon there'll be hell toupee.

Why is it impossible to throw a surprise birthday party for a psychic?
Because they can always sense your presents.

What do you call a sheep on a trampoline?
A woolly jumper.

Did you read about the man who was fired from his job at the clock-making factory, even after all those extra hours he put in?

What did the mother turkey say to her disobedient children?
"If your father could see you now, he'd be turning in his gravy."

What snakes comes as standard on a new car?
Windscreen vipers.

What do you call a parrot in a raincoat?
Polyunsaturated.

"DAD, CAN WE HAVE MY FRIEND TOM FOR DINNER?"

"WELL, OKAY, I SUPPOSE. BUT TO BE HONEST I'D PREFER PIZZA."

I was excited to hear that Apple are soon going to start building homes.
But then I realized they wouldn't have Windows.

Did you hear about the optician who fell into his lens-grinding machine?
He made a spectacle of himself.

What was the name of that boy in your class who turned up for school one morning after spending all night in his parents' garden making a deep hole with a spade?
Oh yes, I remember – Doug.

How do you stop your mouth from freezing over in winter?
Grit your teeth.

Why did the white paint suddenly burst into tears as soon it was put on the bedroom ceiling?
Because it was in a state of high emulsion.

Did you hear about the sensitive burglar?
He takes things personally.

Those tree trimmers did an excellent job.
They deserved to take a bough.

What happened when a 7-foot convict and a 3-foot convict escaped from prison together?
Police searched high and low for them.

When did the motorist first realize that the truck ahead had shed its load of cutlery?
When he came to a fork in the road.

Which big cat should you never play cards with?
A cheetah.

Did you hear about the woman who went to the doctor complaining of a persistent headache? The doctor examined her ears and found dozens of dollar bills. He kept pulling them out until he had $1,999.00.
Then the doctor said, "No wonder you're not feeling two grand!"

My therapist told me I needed to express my emotions more. She said, "You need to learn to vent."
But no matter how hard I tried, you could still see my lips move.

How do you stop a bull from charging?
Take away its credit card.

"SON, WILL YOU MAKE A DOCTOR'S APPOINTMENT FOR ME?"

"SURE, DAD. WHICH DOCTOR?"

"NO, JUST THE REGULAR SORT."

Why would it be bad news if Elon Musk were to be involved in a major scandal?
Because Elongate would be really drawn out.

Did you read that last month the chief executive of Ikea was elected prime minister of Sweden?
He's still assembling his cabinet.

Why did the farmer ride his horse into town?
Because it was too heavy to carry.

My boss yelled at me the other day, "You must be the worst train driver ever! How many trains did you derail last year?"
I replied, "I'm not absolutely sure. It's hard to keep track."

Have you been watching that TV documentary series about how ships are put together?
It's riveting.

What did one racehorse say to the other?
"Your pace is familiar, but I don't remember the mane."

Why was the snooker player who ate only red, blue and pink balls always ill?
He wasn't eating enough greens.

Did you hear about the man who has just been appointed chief executive officer of Old MacDonald's farm?
He's the CIEIO.

I had a nasty accident in my study last week when a pile of heavy books suddenly fell on my head.
I guess I only had my shelf to blame.

"DAD, IS IT OKAY IF I HAVE AN APPLE?"

"ANOTHER ONE? YOU HAD ONE THIS MORNING. THEY DON'T GROW ON TREES, YOU KNOW!"

Why did Beethoven spend all day on the toilet?
He was working on his ninth movement.

Why did the reporters on the local newspaper keep bottles of tomato ketchup, Tabasco and mayonnaise hidden away in the back of their desk drawers?
Because journalists never reveal their sauces.

How do we know that sardines are the most stupid fish in the sea?
Because they climb into cans, close the lid and leave the key outside.

Why did the appendix get dressed up?
Because he heard the doctor was taking him out that night.

What did the bald man say when he received a comb for Christmas?
"Thanks. I'll never part with it."

Why do boys often put on two pairs of thick socks before asking a girl out?
In case they get cold feet.

Did you read that two cheese trucks collided in France?
Apparently there was de Brie everywhere.

You shouldn't allow your children to watch big band performances on TV.
There's too much sax and violins.

Why did the miserable old man take toilet roll to his neighbour's housewarming party?
Because he was a party pooper.

I have an inferiority complex, but it's not a very good one.

If I ever find the doctor who screwed up my limb replacement surgery, I'll kill him with my bear hands.

Did you see that biologists have created immortal frogs by removing their vocal cords?
It means they can never croak.

What extinct creatures were notoriously noisy sleepers?
Dinosnores.

"DAD, THERE'S A MAN AT THE DOOR ASKING FOR A SMALL DONATION TOWARDS THE LOCAL SWIMMING POOL."

"GIVE HIM A GLASS OF WATER."

Why couldn't the beaver get back home?
He couldn't find the dam door.

Did you read the story about the dog that ate nothing but garlic?
Apparently his bark was much worse than his bite.

What did the football manager do when the pitch was flooded?
He brought on the subs.

I went to the doctor and told him I've got a rash.
He said: "I'll be as quick as I can."

What was the name of that boy in your class who kept cutting himself when he first started shaving?
Oh yes, I remember – Nick.

Where do you weigh whales?
At a whale weigh station.

Thanks for explaining the word "many" to me.
It means a lot.

Why did the hospital surgeon write rude words on her patient's plaster cast?
So that she could add insult to injury.

Did you read about the man who was mauled while doing the tango in the zoo's big cat enclosure?
He says it's the last time he's going in for one of those lion dancing competitions.

What do you call a group of rabbits walking backwards?
A receding hare line.

Two parrots are sitting on a perch.
One parrot says to the other: "Can you smell fish?"

What did the judge say when the skunk walked into the courtroom?
"Odour in the court!"

"DAD, WHAT'S THAT BOOK YOU'RE ALWAYS READING?"

"IT'S ABOUT THE HISTORY OF SUPERGLUE. I CAN'T PUT IT DOWN."

Did you hear about the peppermint that became so angry that it burst and started leaking everywhere?
It went absolutely menthol.

When I was a student, my flatmates kept telling me off for borrowing their kitchen utensils.
But it was a whisk I was willing to take.

What is the quickest way to make anti-freeze?
Hide her blanket.

Did you hear about the two thieves who stole a calendar?
They each got six months.

Why are penguins socially awkward at parties?
Because they don't know how to break the ice.

What has four wheels and flies?
A garbage truck.

What did one cannibal say to the other cannibal while they were eating a clown?
"Does this taste funny to you?"

What were the names of those two boys in your class who always used to stand in the window?
Oh yes, I remember – Kurt and Rod.

Did you hear about the man who always kept a clock under his desk so that he could work overtime?

Why did the Norse god of thunder need to stretch his leg muscles so much when he was a child?
Because he was a little Thor.

What is a lawyer's favourite drink?
Subpoena colada.

Which organization combines basket-making and handcrafts with extortion, corruption and murder?
The Raffia.

What did Jay-Z call his wife before they were married?
Feyoncé

Did you hear about the man who got hit in the head with a can of soda?
He was lucky it was a soft drink.

What do you call an elephant that doesn't matter?
An irrelephant.

What did the pirate say on his eightieth birthday?
"Aye, matey."

Every morning I announce to my family that I'm going jogging, but then I don't go.
It's a running joke.

"DAD, HOW DO I LOOK?"

"WITH YOUR EYES."

Did you read that half a dozen police dogs escaped from their handlers, ran off and haven't been seen since?
The police say that at present they don't have any leads.

Why don't photons ever need luggage?
Because they are travelling light.

Why did the tomato turn black and shrivelled after being questioned at the police station?
Because he had been grilled by detectives for over an hour.

Did you hear about the hospital patient whose health has improved dramatically since he had a neck brace fitted last year?
In fact, he hasn't looked back since.

Why did the golfer keep saying: "Hello, Mr Ball, how are you today?"
Because his coach told him he had to address his ball before every shot.

What do you call a hot dog on wheels?
Fast food.

What was the name of that girl in your class who always used to stroll around aimlessly without any real sense of purpose or direction?
Oh yes, I remember – Wanda.

My boss says he has a clean conscience.
But that's only because it's never been used.

Why did the man throw his clock out of the third-floor window?
He wanted to see time fly.

Did you read about these new reversible jackets?
I'll be interested to see how they turn out.

Why did the computer always play "Someone Like You?"
It was a Dell.

What's black and white, black and white, black and white, and black and white?
A penguin rolling down a hill.

"DAD, DO YOU WANT A BOX FOR THE LEFTOVERS?"

"NO, BUT I'LL WRESTLE YOU FOR THEM."

I asked my wife if I was the only one she'd ever slept with. She said: "Yes, the others were all eights and nines."

How do you make a water bed bouncier?
Fill it with spring water.

Did you hear about the two fish in a tank?
One fish says: "How do you drive this thing?"

I spent a lot of time, money and effort childproofing my house.
But the kids still get in.

Why was the fox depressed after killing and eating a young swan?
Because he felt down in the mouth.

What happened when the snowman fell out with his girlfriend?
She gave him the cold shoulder.

Where was King David's temple located?
Just above his ear.

Why did the chimpanzee quit his job at the zoo?
He was fed up with working for peanuts.

Why do Swedish warships have giant barcodes painted on their sides?
To Scandinavian.

People who use selfie sticks really need to take a good, long look at themselves.

What was the name of that boy in your class whose parents named him after two parts of the human body?
Oh yes, I remember – Tony.

Did you read that a Dutchman has invented shoes that record how many miles you've walked?
Clever clogs.

Why did the dock throw itself into the sea?
Pier pressure.

I spent a fortune on hiring a stretch limo, only to learn that it didn't come with a driver.
I can't believe that after spending all that money I've got nothing to chauffeur it.

Why was the calendar afraid?
Its days were numbered.

"DAD, WHAT HAPPENS TO YOU WHEN YOU DIE?"

"WELL, I'VE DECIDED THAT I'M GOING TO BE CREMATED BECAUSE IT WILL BE MY LAST CHANCE TO HAVE A SMOKIN' HOT BODY."

What was the name of that boy in your class who used to do a really good impression of a dog barking?
Oh yes, I remember – Rolf.

Did you read that a truck carrying a consignment of small nails shed its load in the middle of the road, causing the car behind to swerve violently to avoid them?
It seems harsh, but the car driver was charged with tacks evasion.

What has five toes but isn't your foot?
My foot.

What do you call an unemployed jester?
Nobody's fool.

How much does it cost Santa Claus to park his sleigh?
Nothing. It's on the house.

Where would you find a cow with no legs?
Exactly where you left it.

Why was the terrible boxer nicknamed "the Artist"?
Because he spent so much time on the canvas.

Did you read about the hosiery saleswoman who managed to escape uninjured through a third-floor window?
Luckily she found a ladder in her tights.

What do you call a psychic who has a very pudgy face?
A four-chin teller.

What is grey, has large ears, a trunk and squeaks?
An elephant wearing new shoes.

The book on chronology that I ordered has finally arrived.
It's about time...

"DAD, DON'T YOU THINK IT'S BEEN NICE WEATHER FOR MAY AND JUNE?"

"I THINK IT'S BEEN NICE WEATHER FOR EVERYONE."

What do you call an ostrich with its head in the sand?
Anything you want because it can't hear you.

What did the judge say to his dentist?
"I want you to pull my tooth, the whole tooth and nothing but the tooth."

RIP boiled water.
You will be mist.

On which side of their bodies do chickens have the most feathers?
On the outside.

Did you read about the artist who wrongly believed that his favourite colour of paint had been stolen?
It turned out to be just a pigment of his imagination.

How did the police manage to locate a suspect standing on a set of bathroom scales?
He gave himself a weigh.

Why is it dangerous to eat Christmas tree decorations?
Because you might get tinselitis.

Which ancient fruit launched a thousand ships?
Melon of Troy.

Did you see that they've installed an undersea phone box off the coast of Florida?
Everyone who uses it is ringing wet.

My wife says she's leaving me because I'm totally obsessed with astronomy.
What planet is she on?!

"DAD, WHAT DO YOU THINK IS HOLDING ME BACK?"

"WELL, I'M NO ANATOMIST, BUT I'D SAY IT'S YOUR SPINE."

What was the name of that girl in your class who could never do metric conversions?
Oh yes, I remember – Lolita.

How can you recognize a dogwood tree?
By its bark.

Did you hear about the army karate champion?
The first time he saluted, he nearly killed himself.

What did the extremely shy pebble say to its friend?
"I wish I was a little boulder."

Why did the aristocratic lady turn down the gardener's proposal of marriage?
She thought he was too rough around the hedges.

What's the fastest vegetable?
A runner bean.

Did you know that Count Dracula was eventually killed by a barrage of sausage rolls, vol-au-vents and sandwiches?
They think it was the work of Buffet the Vampire Slayer.

Why did the airplane pilot crash into the house?
Because the landing lights were on.

To the person who invented the zero, thanks for nothing.

Why did the pigeons join the army?
To stage a military coo.

Did you read about the man who jumped off a bridge in Paris?
He was found in Seine.

My wife wanted to know whether I was ever going to grow out of my obsession for singing Oasis songs.
I said: "Maybe..."

"DAD, DO YOU THINK MY LATEST BOYFRIEND IS A KEEPER?"

"I DON'T KNOW. IS HE ANY GOOD AT SAVING PENALTIES?"

Did you read about the man who went to the doctor's with a piece of lettuce sticking out of his ear?
When the doctor looked concerned, the man said: "It gets worse. That's just the tip of the iceberg."

What's the difference between weather and climate?
You can't weather a tree but you can climate.

What was the name of that girl in your class who loved kebabs?
Oh yes, I remember – Donna.

I wanted to read an online synopsis of that new film about high-performance sports cars.
But then I realized there were spoilers.

Did you know that Ireland's capital has the fastest-growing population in the whole world?
Every day it's Dublin.

Why do fish live in salt water?
Because pepper makes them sneeze.

Why did the lobster blush?
Because it saw the ocean's bottom.

Did you read about the guy who was riding a motorbike along a country lane when his girlfriend, Ruth, who was riding pillion, fell off? He didn't even stop. He just rode on.
Absolutely ruthless.

I told my wife she should embrace her mistakes.
She gave me a hug.

Why do gorillas have big nostrils?
Because they have big fingers.

What's the difference between Batman and a shoplifter?
Batman can go into a store without Robin.

Why was the solicitor left red-faced in court?
Not only had he neglected to put on any trousers, but he had also forgotten his briefs.

I built a model of Mount Everest. My son asked if it was to scale.
I said: "No, it's to look at."

"HAVE YOU HEARD THE JOKE ABOUT THE FAIRY CALLED NUFF?"

"NO, DAD, I HAVEN'T."

"FAIRY NUFF."

Did you hear about the toddler who refused to take a nap?
She was charged with resisting a rest.

Why did the young offender steal a ladder?
He was told he needed to take steps to avoid going back to prison.

How is an exhausted kangaroo like a wayward shot on a golf course?
Both are out of bounds.

What was the name of that girl in your class whose father was a tough corporate lawyer?
Oh yes, I remember – Sue.

Did you hear about the man who put on a clean pair of socks every day?
By the end of the week he couldn't get his shoes on.

Why is the sky so high?
So that birds don't bump their heads.

Two monkeys are climbing into a bath. One goes: "Ooh, ooh, ah, ah, ah, ah, ah."
The other says: "Well, put some cold in then."

I bought a new mouse mat today.

Hopefully that will stop them leaving footprints all over the kitchen floor.

What did Prince get when he crossed a zucchini with a beetroot?
A little red courgette.

I went for a Covid test, and the doctor asked me if I had experienced a sudden loss of taste.
I said: "No, I always dress like this."

"DAD, HAVE YOU EVER TRIED TO WRITE A SONG?"

"I ONCE WROTE A SONG ABOUT A TORTILLA, BUT TO BE HONEST IT WAS MORE OF A RAP."

Did you read about the tomb they recently discovered in Egypt that was filled with hazelnuts and chocolate?
Archaeologists believe it belonged to Pharaoh Rocher.

When your mum finds out that I've replaced our bed with a trampoline, she'll hit the roof.

Who do bees have sticky hair?
Because they use a honeycomb.

If you think swimming with dolphins is expensive, try swimming with sharks.
It cost me an arm and a leg.

What did the duck say when she purchased a new lipstick?
"Put it on my bill."

Did you hear about the glassblower who accidentally inhaled?
He got a pane in the stomach.

What did the bartender say when Bono and the Edge walked into the bar?
"Oh no, not U2 again!"

What do you call a snobby criminal walking down the steps?
A condescending con descending.

What's the difference between a photocopier and the flu?
One makes facsimiles and the other makes sick families.

Did you hear about the man who went into a shop to buy some camouflage trousers?
He couldn't find any.

What do you call a pig that performs karate?
A pork chop.

Just lately I've been spending a lot of time admiring the ceiling in my living-room.
I'm not sure if it's the best ceiling in the street, but it's definitely up there.

What was the name of that boy in your class who loved walking over dry leaves?
Oh yes, I remember – Russell.

Did you read about the soldier who survived mustard gas and pepper spray?
He's now a seasoned veteran.

"DAD, HAVE YOU SEEN MY SUNGLASSES?"

"NO, SON. HAVE YOU SEEN MY DAD GLASSES?"

Why do milking stools have only three legs?
Because the cow's got the udder.

Why did the cucumber cry out for help?
It was in a pickle.

One of my favourite things is when the Earth rotates.
It makes my day.

What did the woodcutter's wife say to her husband in December?
"Not many chopping days left until Christmas."

Did you read about the man who used to be addicted to the hokey cokey?
But then he turned himself around.

What do you call a horse that is more bashful than the other horses?
A shire horse.

A piece of string walks into a bar but the bartender says: "We don't serve pieces of string here."
So the string goes outside, ruffles his hair and tries again. The bartender looks at him and says, "Aren't you that piece of string who came in just now?"
"No," said the string, "I'm a frayed knot."

Did you read about the boy who kept chewing on electrical wires?
It got so bad that his dad had to ground him.

When I was younger, I learned to pick locks and I must say, it's opened a lot of doors for me.

Did you read about the man who was found dead in a vat of cornflakes?
He was the victim of a cereal killer.

What do you call a book club that has been stuck on one book for years?
Church.

"DAD, THERE'S A GIRL AT SCHOOL WHO CAN PLAY PIANO BY EAR."

"I BET SHE'D FIND IT EASIER IF SHE USED HER HANDS."

Have you heard about the new charity movement to help citrus fruit?
It's called Lemon Aid.

Why did the circus lion eat the tightrope walker?
Because he wanted a well-balanced diet.

My friend Jack claims that he can communicate with vegetables.
Yes, Jack and the beans talk.

Why didn't the witch ride her broomstick to her anger-management classes?
In case she flew off the handle.

What was the name of that girl in your class who used to wear two slices of tomato, a lettuce leaf, shredded onion and a burger bun on her head?
Oh yes, I remember – Patty.

Did you read about the couple who split up because the boy refused to take out a gym membership?
His girlfriend said it was clear the two of them were never going to work out.

What kind of cheese could you hide a small horse in?
Mascarpone.

Why did the young man decide to quit tap dancing?
Because he kept falling in the sink.

Why was the restaurant customer served a crustacean wearing a miniature tuxedo and bow tie?
He had ordered dressed lobster.

So what if I don't know the meaning of the word "apocalypse".
It's not the end of the world.

Why do oysters never give to charity?
Because they're shellfish.

"GO ON, DAD, TELL ME A JOKE. I KNOW YOU CAN'T RESIST IT."

"WELL, I HEARD A FUNNY ONE ABOUT A BOOMERANG THE OTHER DAY. I CAN'T REMEMBER IT AT THE MOMENT BUT I'M SURE IT WILL COME BACK TO ME."

What was the name of that boy in your class who always used to wear two raincoats?
Oh yes, I remember – Max.

Did you read about the editor who denied leaving her work in the kitchen?
But the proof was in the pudding.

What do you get if you cross a woodpecker and a carrier pigeon?
A bird that knocks before it delivers a message.

Did you hear about the cat that ate a piece of cheese and then waited for a mouse with baited breath?

Why did the farmer call his pig "Ink"?
Because it was always running out of the pen.

I used to get small electric shocks when touching certain objects, but recently it stopped.
Needless to say, I'm ex-static.

Why are giraffes slow to apologize?
Because it takes them a long time to swallow their pride.

Did you read about the French museum that displayed a baguette in a cage?
It was bread in captivity.

I asked the company IT guy: "How do you make a motherboard?"
He said: "I tell her about my job."

"DAD, WHY HAVEN'T YOU GIVEN ME ANY PEAS WITH DINNER?"

"HAVEN'T YOU HEARD THE EXPRESSION: NO PEAS FOR THE WICKED?"

Did you know that the man who invented the crossword puzzle was once treated for depression?
His therapist told him not to get two down.

Why do birds fly south in the winter?
Because it's faster than walking.

Just because I don't like soap, there's no need to rub it in my face.

Why did the World Wildlife Fund choose the giant panda as their symbol?
Because they didn't have a colour printer.

In the boxing ring, what was the difference between Evander Holyfield and Mike Tyson?
One was champing at the bit, the other was biting at the champ.

Why was the computer exhausted when it got home?
Because it had a hard drive.

Did you see that Bob the Builder has emigrated and set up business on a French island in the Mediterranean? Can he fix it?
Corsican!

I used to date a girl with a lazy eye.
It turned out she was seeing someone else the whole time.

Where do pumpkins go to settle their differences?
A squash court.

What happened to the exorcist when he had a cash flow problem?
His car got repossessed.

What did Adam say on 24 December?
"It's Christmas, Eve."

Did you read that the sexy human organ thief has finally been arrested?
It seems she stole one heart too many.

I asked the doctor if he could give me something for persistent wind.
He suggested a kite.

"DAD, I GOT A NEW ELECTRIC TOASTER FOR MUM."

"SOUNDS LIKE A GOOD TRADE."

What was the name of that girl in your class who never understood what separated the two halves of a tennis court?
Oh yes, I remember – Annette.

To the person who stole my Microsoft Office, I will find you.
You have my Word.

What's the easiest way to burn a thousand calories?
Leave the pizza in the oven.

How do you get a ghost to lie perfectly flat?
You use a spirit level.

Did you read about the guy who has become addicted to drinking brake fluid?
He says it's okay. He can stop whenever he wants.

My phone rang the other day and all I could hear was chattering teeth and someone shivering.
I reckon it was a cold caller.

What animals didn't enter the Ark in a pair?
The worms, because they went in an apple.

I was chatting to a scarecrow the other day. He said: "This job isn't for everyone but, hay, it's in my jeans."

What's the difference between bird flu and swine flu?
One requires tweetment and the other requires an oinkment.

Where do vampires keep their savings?
In blood banks.

Did you read about the rumours of a food shortage at this year's World Spoonerism Convention?
It turned out to be a complete lack of pies.

What do you call a cow with a twitch?
Beef jerky.

I've been thinking about learning Braille, but it's a bit of a touchy subject.

What's the difference between Santa Claus and a dog?
Santa Claus wears a whole suit, a dog just pants.

I've just been informed by the optometrist that I'm colour-blind.
The news came completely out of the purple.

"DAD, HOW DO YOU ALWAYS MANAGE TO FALL ASLEEP SO QUICKLY AFTER SUNDAY LUNCH?"

"FALLING ASLEEP IS EASY. I CAN DO IT WITH MY EYES CLOSED."

Why are whales so intelligent?
Because they spend all day in schools.

Did you hear about the dry cleaner who was arrested?
Apparently he was laundering money.

Not to boast, but I made six figures last year.
I was also named the slowest employee at the toy factory.

Why did the nurse need a red pen?
In case he needed to draw blood.

I contacted a handyman and gave him a list of jobs to do around the house, but he only did jobs one, three and five.
It turns out he only does odd jobs.

What always succeeds?
A toothless budgie.

Why did the elderly man steal six iPads from the computer store?
His doctor had told him to keep taking the tablets.

What do you get if you lie under a cow?
A pat on the head.

Did you read about the parents who got fed up with having to sew name tags into their son's school shirts?
They decided to change his name by deed poll to "Machine Washable".

My friend David is a victim of ID theft.
So now everyone just calls him Dav.

People are often shocked when they find out I'm not a very good electrician.

"DAD, THERE'S A HOLE IN MY SHOE. I NEED NEW ONES."

"THERE'S A HOLE IN MINE, TOO, SON. THAT'S HOW I GET MY FOOT INSIDE."

Have you seen the optometrist's new web page?
It's a site for sore eyes.

What was the name of that girl in your class whose parents used to tie her up by rope to a jetty?
Oh yes, I remember – Maud.

Why did the teddy bear say no to dessert?
Because it was stuffed.

Did you read about the man who went to the doctor's because he was convinced that he was shrinking?
The doctor told him that any cure would take six months to work and in the meantime he would have to be a little patient.

What do you call a factory that makes okay products?
A satisfactory.

I tried to explain to my four-year-old son that it's perfectly normal to accidentally poop your pants.
But he still makes fun of me.

Do you know why the famous Olympic athlete decided to retire from competitive skiing?
Her career was going downhill.

What do you get if you cross a kangaroo with an elephant?
Great big holes all over Australia.

Why did the golfer refuse an offer of water before teeing off?
Because you should never drink and drive.

Did you hear about the dietician who is on a crusade to tell the public about the benefits of eating dried grapes?
He says it's all about raisin awareness.

I can cut down a tree using nothing but my vision. It's true. I saw it with my own eyes.

"DAD, DID YOU PUT THE CAT OUT?"

"I DIDN'T NEED TO. IT WASN'T ON FIRE."

Did you hear about the man who was fired from his job in the orange juice factory?
He couldn't concentrate.

Why do companies like to hire people who suffer from claustrophobia?
Because they're better at thinking outside the box.

Why did the cowboy wear a chocolate bar as a hat?
There was a bounty on his head.

I just read that alligators can grow up to 15 feet.
But I've never seen any with more than four.

What's the difference between a vegetable grower and a pool player?
One minds his peas, the other minds his cues.

My brother is a wealthy businessman who has made his fortune from manufacturing and selling refrigerators.
Put simply, he's a fridge magnate.

Who did the trout, the pike and the salmon consult to improve their mobility underwater?
The orthopaedic sturgeon.

Shall I tell you one thing that always makes me throw up?
A dart board on the ceiling.

What do you call a man with two left feet?
You can call him whatever you like. If he tries to catch you, he'll just run around in circles.

What's worse than raining cats and dogs?
Hailing taxis.

I had to quit my job as a personal trainer because the gym boss said I wasn't strong enough.
So I handed in my too weak notice.

I'm not saying you put on too much perfume.
I'm just saying the canary was alive before you walked into the room.

"DAD, CAN YOU KEEP A SECRET?"

"ABSOLUTELY. I'M GREAT AT KEEPING SECRETS. IT'S THE PEOPLE I TELL THEM TO THAT CAN'T."

What's blue and smells like red paint?
Blue paint.

Have you heard about the new sport called quiet tennis?
It's like normal tennis but without the racket.

What did the postcard say to the stamp?
"Stick with me and we'll go places."

Did you read about the man who accidentally swallowed a stack of Scrabble tiles?
His next trip to the bathroom could spell disaster.

Why did the solicitor bring a ladder to the courtroom?
Because she wanted to take the case to a higher court.

It's a five-minute walk from my house to the pub, but a 25-minute walk from the pub to my house.
The difference is staggering.

Why are photographers so depressed?
Because they're always focusing on the negatives.

I think my wife is secretly smearing glue on my antique firearms collection.
Of course she denies it, but I'm sticking to my guns.

"DAD, YOU'RE LOOKING A BIT DIZZY. HAVE YOU GOT VERTIGO?"

"NO, ONLY ABOUT ANOTHER 50 YARDS."

What did the left eye say to the right eye?
"Between you and me, something smells."

What did the Beach Boys say when they walked into the bar?
"Round, round, round, round, I get a round..."

Last week, I was doing 40 in a 30-mile-an-hour zone when a blond-haired police officer stopped me for speeding.
It was a fair cop.

How did the lumberjack know that he had chopped down precisely 62,791 trees in the course of his long career?
Because he always kept a log.

Did you hear about the man who went to a farm to buy a dozen bees?
He was given 13 instead and when he pointed that there was one too many, he was told it was a freebie.

What is over 300 metres high, located in France and made of iron, fruit, jelly and sponge?
The Trifle Tower.

Do you know what the leading cause of dry skin is?
Towels.

What was the name of that girl in your class whose laugh always sounded like a horse neighing?
Oh yes, I remember – Winnie.

Did you hear about the man who fell into the infinity pool?
It took him forever to get out.

What do you call a chicken on a skateboard?
Poultry in motion.

Why has Santa Claus been banned from climbing down sooty chimneys?
Because of his carbon footprints.

What's the difference between pizza and your opinion?
I asked for the pizza.

"DAD, THERE'S A BEETLE CRAWLING ACROSS THE FLOOR."

"IS IT PAUL OR RINGO?"

What do you call a blind deer?
No eye deer.

My wife has left me because of my obsession with pasta.
I'm feeling cannelloni right now.

What's the difference between a buffalo and a bison?
You can't wash your hands in a buffalo.

Did you read about the man who ate yeast and shoe polish so that every day he could rise and shine?

What do you call a cow during an earthquake?
A milkshake.

It's always worth dating a contortionist.
They'll bend over backwards to please you.

What pirate can't stop rivulets of drool falling from his mouth?
Long John Saliva.

Who is the coolest doctor in the hospital?
The hip consultant.

Did you read that engineers have successfully built cars that can run on parsley?
Now they're trying to develop trains that can run on thyme.

How many tickles does it take to make an octopus laugh?
Ten tickles.

Why is there no official training for trash collectors?
Because they just pick things up as they go along.

Did you hear about the woman who dreamed she was eating a giant marshmallow?
When she woke up the next morning, her pillow was gone.

My three favourite things are eating my family and not using commas.

Have you heard about that new band called 999 Megabytes?
They're good, but they still haven't got a gig yet.

I'm friends with 25 letters of the alphabet.
I don't know Y.

"DAD, HAVE YOU SEEN THE DOG BOWL?"

"TO BE HONEST, I DIDN'T EVEN KNOW HE PLAYED."

Did you read about the man who took his laptop to the beach and then flooded it with sea water?
He was trying to surf the internet.

What is stubborn, has four legs, tilts at windmills and is friends with Sancho Panza?
Donkey Hote.

Why should bananas wear sun cream?
To stop them from peeling.

Be kind to dentists.
They have fillings too, you know.

What's brown and sticky?
A stick.

When I turned 21, my dad took me to one side, put his arm around my shoulders and said to me: "Son, when I was your age, I was 21."

Why do demons and ghouls get along so well?
Because demons are a ghoul's best friend.

Did you hear about the email that was circulating and which claimed that you could catch swine flu through eating tinned pork and ham?
People were advised not to open it because it was just spam.

When five cows and a chicken turned up for an audition for the percussion section in a new rock band, why was the chicken the successful applicant?
He was the only one with drumsticks.

I put up a high-voltage electric fence around my property over the weekend.
My neighbour is dead against it.

Did you see that there's a collection of broken puppets for sale on eBay?
The ad must be genuine because it reads "No strings attached".

"DAD, WHY HAVE YOU GOT A BEARD?"

"IT'S FUNNY BECAUSE I NEVER USED TO BE A FAN OF FACIAL HAIR. BUT THEN IT STARTED TO GROW ON ME."

Why was the baby strawberry crying?
Because its parents were in a jam.

What was the name of that girl in your class who used to do a great impression of a police car siren?
Oh yes, I remember – Nina.

Did you read about the taxi driver who has a terrible fear of speed bumps?
He's slowly getting over it.

Guess who I bumped into on my way to the optician's to get my glasses fixed?
Everybody!

What did the male octopus say to the female octopus?
"I want to hold your hand, hand, hand, hand, hand, hand, hand, hand."

Why did the man put his money in the freezer?
Because he wanted cold, hard cash.

Did you watch that TV documentary about life in the Royal Navy?
The ratings were good.

Why did the parents decide to call both of their sons Edward?
Because two Eds are better than one.

My wife keeps telling me to stop pretending to be butter.
But I'm on a roll now.

What's blue and not very heavy?
Light blue.

What did Leif Eriksen's wife say to the Swedish authorities after her husband's name was omitted from the national population count?
"You must have taken Leif off your census!"

Did you see that the man who owned the ice cream van in the park died last week?
Apparently there were hundreds and thousands at his funeral.

When the doctor told me I was very sick, I asked for a second opinion.
He said: "You're ugly, too."

"DAD, *I NEED A* PASSWORD EIGHT CHARACTERS LONG."

"HOW ABOUT SNOW WHITE AND THE SEVEN DWARFS?"

Did you know that milk is the fastest liquid on Earth?
It's pasteurized before you can even see it.

My landlord said he wanted to talk to me about the size of my heating bill. I told him:
"Anytime. My door is always open."

What was even more useful than the first telephone?
The second telephone.

Where do you learn to make ice cream?
At sundae school.

Did you hear about the man who lost his job as a bank cashier?
A customer asked him to check her balance, so he pushed her over.

My friend asked me to round up his 48 sheep.
I said, "50."

Did you know that diarrhoea is hereditary?
Yes, it runs in your jeans.

I went to the library this morning and asked if they had any books about paranoia.
"Yes," said the librarian, "they're right behind you."

Why did the young man decide not to apply for a job as a cemetery worker?
Because he had grave concerns.

Where did Napoleon keep his armies?
Up his sleevies.

Did you hear about the man who thought he was becoming a kleptomaniac?
The doctor suggested he take something for it.

And God said to John: "Come forth and you shall be granted eternal life."
But John came fifth and won a toaster.

I asked my boss: "Where do you want me to put this 10-metre roll of bubble wrap?"
He said: "Just pop it in the corner." It took me six hours...

What was the name of that boy at your school who used to walk around with a seagull on his head?
Oh yes, I remember – Cliff.

"DAD, MY WRIST IS REALLY SORE."

"I THINK WE'LL HAVE TO TAKE YOU TO A SECOND-HAND SHOP."

Did you read about the man who was ordered by the council to destroy the ten wooden panels and posts that he had stored in his garden ready for use?
The council said the items were likely to cause a fence.

Did you hear what happened to the human cannonball?
He got fired.

But why did the human cannonball soon get his old job back?
Because they couldn't find another man of his calibre.

What's the difference between Joan of Arc and a canoe?

One was Maid of Orleans, the other is made of wood.

I'm renovating the house.

The first floor is going great, but the second floor is another storey.

What did the slow tomato say to the other tomatoes?

"Don't worry, I'll ketchup."

While in a supermarket, why should you not go up to the fish counter?

Because it will interrupt him, and he'll have to start all over again.

Why did the man give up trying to read a book about the history of Sellotape?

Because he couldn't find the beginning.

Did you read about the new type of broom that has come out? Apparently it's really popular.

It's sweeping the nation.

Why is it sad that parallel lines have so much in common?
Because they'll never meet.

I used to go out with a girl called Claire Lee at the same time as I was living with another girl called Lorraine. But last week Lorraine found out and dumped me, which is great because it means...
I can see Claire Lee now Lorraine has gone.

"DAD, I'M GOING TO TAKE A SHOWER."

"MAKE SURE YOU PUT IT BACK AFTERWARDS."

What do you get if you cross a parrot with a pig?
A bird that always hogs the conversation.

Did you hear about the two silkworms who had a race?
It ended in a tie.

Today my son asked, "Can I have a book mark?" and I just burst into tears.
Twelve years old and he still doesn't know my name is Keith.

Why was the medieval king's army very tired?
They had too many sleepless knights.

What would you do if you found yourself surrounded by eight lions, eight tigers, eight elephants, eight giraffes, eight kangaroos and eight hippopotamuses?
Step off the fairground carousel.

Why did the New York garage mechanic spend the night sleeping under a car?
Because he had to wake up oily.

When lightning strikes an orchestra, who is the most likely to get hit?
The conductor.

What's the difference between a Boy Scout and someone whose job is fixing car horns?
One's motto is "Be prepared" and the other's is "Beep repaired".

What did the green grape say to the purple grape?
"Stay calm! Breathe! Breathe!"

Did you read about the man who adopted a dog from a blacksmith?
As soon as he brought it home it made a bolt for the door.

What do you call a magician who's lost his magic?
Ian.

"DAD, WHY DO FRENCH PEOPLE EAT SNAILS?"

"BECAUSE THEY DON'T LIKE FAST FOOD."

What did the three-legged dog say when he walked into a Wild West saloon?
"I'm looking for the man who shot my paw."

Just as I suspected, someone added yet more soil to my garden last night. The plot thickens.

What was the name of that girl in your class who was always very good at keeping secrets?
Oh yes, I remember – Chantelle.

Did you hear about the man who kept getting heartburn whenever he ate birthday cake?
The doctor suggested that in future he should try blowing out the candles first.

What do you call a sheep with no legs?
A cloud.

Why were the recently divorced couple throwing a sweet yellowy mixture of milk and eggs at each other?
Because they were in the middle of a custardy battle.

How do you get Pikachu on a bus?
You poke him on.

Why didn't the chef in the Chinese restaurant know what to do for the best when he became trapped next to the kitchen wall?
Because he was caught between a wok and a hard place.

What do you call a wizard on a plane?
A flying sorcerer.

Why did the boat sink while it was carrying a cargo of vegetables?
Because there were a lot of leeks on the lower deck.

Is it okay to plant an explosive device inside a male cow?
No, it's abombinabull.

My dad suggested that I should register for a donor card.
He's a man after my own heart.

Did you read about the detective who thought he had discovered the mass grave of a thousand snowmen?
It turned out to be a carrot field.

How many squares are there on a chess board?
Two plus the spectators.

Last month I went on a once-in-a-lifetime holiday.
Never again.

"DAD, WHERE ARE THE HIMALAYAS?"

"IF YOU PUT THINGS AWAY, YOU'D KNOW WHERE TO FIND THEM."

Did you hear about the man who lost his job as a shoe salesman?
The company gave him the boot.

Why did the little girl put lipstick on her forehead?
She was trying to make up her mind.

Why did the owner of the dolphinarium reject the delivery of rotting fish?
Because he decided they were not fit for porpoise.

What's the difference between roast pork and pea soup?
You can roast pork...

Did you read about the scientist who created a liquid so corrosive that it could burn through any material?
He spent the rest of his life trying to invent a container to hold it in.

I went into a pet shop to buy a goldfish. The shop owner said: "Do you want an aquarium?"
I said: "I don't care what star sign it is."

Did you see that the police were called out to the World Gurning Championships at the weekend?
Apparently things had started to turn ugly.

How do you organize a space party?
You planet.

Someone broke into my house last night and stole my limbo stick?
How can anyone stoop so low?

"DAD, WHAT DO YOU KNOW ABOUT THE DEAD SEA?"

"I DIDN'T EVEN KNOW IT WAS SICK."

Apparently Rick Astley will let you borrow any movie from his Pixar collection except one.
He's never gonna give you Up.

Did you hear about the man who went to the paper shop one morning, only to find it had blown away?

Do you know why the world's leading food taster quit his job?
He had too much on his plate.

Which farmer sits on his tractor, wailing: "The end is nigh. The end is nigh."?
Farmer Geddon.

I broke up with one girlfriend after discovering that she was a communist.
I should have seen it earlier; there were red flags everywhere.

What was the name of that Russian girl in your class who was always scruffily dressed?
Oh yes, I remember – Tatiana.

Did you read about the man who tried to organize a hide-and-seek tournament?
He eventually had to give up because good players were hard to find.

What did the pirate say when his obese parrot died?
"It's sad news, but it's a huge weight off my shoulders."

Why did the young office clerk throw diced pickles, onions and tomatoes at the stack of paperwork on his desk?
Because his boss told him to attack it with relish.

Why did the police officer spend all day in bed beneath the duvet?
He was working undercover.

Did you hear about the hungry clock?
It went back four seconds.

Some people say I'm self-centred.
But enough about them.

What was the name of that boy in your class who eloped with his girlfriend and pleaded with the registrar to give them an instant wedding?
Oh yes, I remember – Marius.

Why should you never tell a secret on a farm?
Because the potatoes have eyes and the corn has ears.

What's the best way to make a bandstand?
Take away their chairs.

"DAD, WHY ARE THERE SO MANY CARS AT THE CEMETERY?"

"IT'S BECAUSE THAT CEMETERY IS REALLY POPULAR. PEOPLE ARE DYING TO GET IN."

Did you read about the man who lived a secret life as a priest?
It was his altar ego.

What's the difference between in-laws and outlaws?
Outlaws are wanted.

I've had my favourite armchair for more than 20 years.
Yes, me and my recliner go way back.

Did you read about the man who passed out after eating too much curry?
He ended up in a korma.

I used to have a job collecting fallen leaves.
I was raking it in.

"DAD, I'VE JUST FINISHED BAKING SOME COOKIES. WOULD YOU LIKE TO TAKE YOUR PICK?"

"NO. I THINK I'LL JUST USE THE HAMMER AS USUAL."

Did you read about the man who bought his wife a pack of playing cards for her birthday?
When he had asked her what she wanted as a gift, she had said, "Anything with diamonds."

What do you get when you cross a snowman with a vampire?
Frostbite.

A colleague at the office told me to cheer up. "It could be worse," he said. "You could be trapped in a deep hole filled with water."
I know he meant well.

What musical instrument do you find in the bathroom?
A tuba toothpaste.

I was surprised when the seller accepted my offer of a root vegetable in exchange for a set of encyclopaedias.
It was a turnip for the books.

What was the name of that boy in your class who was really loud?
Oh yes, I remember – Mike.

Did you read about the office worker who, over a period of 20 years, was only ever ill between Mondays and Fridays?
Doctors eventually discovered that he had a weekend immune system.

Why do toadstools grow so close together?
Because they don't need mushroom.

I asked the hospital surgeon if I could administer my own anaesthetic.
He said: "Sure. Go ahead. Knock yourself out."

"DAD, LAST WEEK THE GUY ACROSS THE ROAD GAVE ME A HORRIBLE LOOK."

"I SEE YOU DECIDED TO KEEP IT."

What do you call a bear with no teeth?
A gummy bear.

Did you read about the man who was bedridden with stomach cramps after eating an apple a day?
The doctor wouldn't come out to see him.

What did one wall say to the other wall?
"I'll meet you at the corner."

What do you call a school principal who keeps a bad-tempered koala as a pet?
A head with a sore bear.

I'm upset because someone has glued my pack of cards together.
I don't know how to deal with it.

What did the tourist guide say as her coach travelled around the Luxembourg ring road?
"We're now going to pass the Duchy on the left-hand side."

Did you hear about the man who accidentally swallowed a dictionary and was worried that he would have to pay for it?
The doctor advised him not to breathe a word to anyone.

I once paid 20 dollars to see Prince in concert.
But I partied like it was $19.99.

What's the best thing about Switzerland?
I don't know, but the flag is a big plus.

What was the name of that boy in your class who wasn't interested in any form of religion?
Oh yes, I remember – Godfrey.

Did you hear about the farmer who couldn't keep his hands off his young wife?
So he fired them.

My wife blocked me on Facebook because I kept posting too many bird puns.
Well, toucan play at that game.

What do you call someone who pretends to be your dad?
A faux pa.

Did you read about what happened at the World Darts Championship? A guy threw a single 20 with his first dart, a treble 20 with his second dart, but then his third dart went straight through the heart of Sister Mary from the convent who was sitting on the front row.
And the announcer called out: "One nun dead and 80!"

To the person who stole my place in the queue.
I'm after you now.

Why did the students try to kill as many flies as they could?
They were swatting for their exams.

"DAD, DO YOU KNOW OF ANY AUTHORS WHO WRITE NOVELS ABOUT DINOSAURS?"

"TRY SARAH TOPPS."

What's the difference between a soldier and a firefighter?
You can't dip a firefighter into your boiled egg.

I told my doctor that I could hear a constant buzzing sound.
"Don't worry," he said, "it's just a bug that's going around."

Did you see that the bakery in town has been forced to close down?
Apparently the business just wasn't making enough dough.

What is black and white and has 16 wheels?
A zebra on roller skates.

What do you get when a chicken looks at a salad?
Chicken sees a salad.

Did you see that a prison van collided with a cement mixer on the highway?
The police are on the lookout for 12 hardened criminals.

What's the difference between a man with an unnaturally high voice and a man with dentures?
One has a falsetto voice and the other has a false set o' teeth.

As I handed my dad his eightieth birthday card, he looked at me with tears in his eyes and said: "You know, son, one would have been enough."

Have you seen the price of Velcro these days?
What a rip-off!

Have you read about the new reality TV show to find the country's best osteopath?
It's called Bone Idol.

For the first time in months, I attended a meeting of Cosmetic Surgery Addicts Anonymous.
I saw a lot of new faces there.

"DAD, WILL YOU PUT KETCHUP ON THE SHOPPING LIST?"

"OKAY, BUT I MIGHT NOT BE ABLE TO READ IT AFTERWARDS."

Why can you never hear a psychiatrist go to the toilet?
Because the "pee" is silent.

Did you read that detectives are hunting a gang of thieves who have been stealing all the rubber off police car wheels?
They say they're working tirelessly to find the culprits.

Do you think people are born with a photographic memory or does it take time to develop?

What was the name of that girl in your class who used to spend most weekends cutting her dad's lawn?
Oh yes, I remember – Mo.

I see that Disney are releasing a new film that contains excessive cursing.
It's called 101 Damnations.

I said to the taxi driver: "King George's Close."
He said: "Don't worry, we'll lose him at the next set of lights."

Did you hear about the man who was sitting outside at a restaurant when it suddenly started raining heavily?
It took him in an hour and a half to finish his soup.

How many ears does Captain Kirk have?
Three. The left ear, the right ear and the final front ear.

Why do bookshops contain so many baseball autobiographies?
Because every pitcher tells a story.

"DAD, IF YOU COULD HAVE ANY SUPERPOWER IN THE WORLD, WHAT WOULD IT BE?"

"CHINA."

Why was the kitchen designer arrested?
Because police suspected he was a counter fitter.

For an actor, breaking a leg during an audition always guarantees that you end up in the cast.

Did you read about the young man who went to a seafood disco and pulled a mussel?

When it comes to maths, I can just about tolerate algebra, maybe even a few logarithms, but geometry is where I draw the line.

Did you hear about the man who phoned Gamblers Anonymous for help with his addiction to playing fruit machines?
They asked him if he wanted to hold.

What's the difference between a boxer and a man with a cold?
One knows his blows and the other blows his nose.

My feet were so sore, I went to see the new chiropodist in town. I must say he's very good.
He certainly knows his bunions.

How do we know that woodpeckers are smarter than chickens?
Ever heard of Kentucky Fried Woodpecker?

Did you read about the man who was crushed to death by a falling piano?
His funeral was very low key.

Most people know about the philosopher Karl Marx, but no one ever remembers his sister Onya, the inventor of the starting pistol.

Did you watch that TV documentary about shovels?
It was real ground-breaking stuff.

What were the names of those two kids in your class who suffered a nasty bout of food poisoning after a school trip?
Oh yes, I remember – Sam 'n' Ella.

Did you hear about the dyslexic zombie?
It only eats Brians.

Someone stole the plug off the kettle at work today.
I can see trouble brewing.

"SORRY ABOUT YOUR WAIT, DAD."

"ARE YOU SAYING I'M FAT?"

What did the police officer say to her belly button?
"You're under a vest."

Why did the restaurant waiter bring the customer a pair of dentures in a glass?
Because the customer had clicked his fingers and ordered "aperitif".

I once went out with identical twins named Earth and Water.
But I soon discovered their names were mud around here.

What do you call werewolves who don't know that they're werewolves?
Unawarewolves.

Did you read about the man who developed a taste for fabric conditioner?
His doctor told him it's just Comfort eating.

I must admit I was a little jealous when I saw my friend holding hands with a giant lollipop and a big box of chocolates.
Then I realized they were just arm candy.

Why were the elephants thrown out of the public swimming pool?
They kept lowering their trunks.

What was the name of that girl in your class who had a really hairy top lip?
Oh yes, I remember – Tash.

Why did the mother kangaroo jump up and down?
Because she caught the kids smoking in bed.

Did you hear about the couple who met at a summer fair?
Fête brought them together.

What do you get if you cross a centipede with a parrot?
A walkie-talkie.

I always keep emergency flares in my car.
Because you never know when you're going to be invited to a 1970s disco.

Did you read about the cat that ate a ball of wool?
She had mittens.

'DAD, IS IT TRUE THAT BABIES ARE DELIVERED BY STORKS?'

'WELL, SMALLER BABIES MAY BE DELIVERED BY STORK BUT HEAVIER ONES NEED A CRANE.'

I was absolutely furious with the thieves who broke into my farm last week and stole my prize-winning nanny.
They really got my goat.

What's the difference between people in Dubai and Abu Dhabi?
People in Dubai don't like the Flintstones but people in Abu Dhabi do!

What do you call a beehive with no exit?
Unbelievable.

Did you hear about the man who started chatting up a cheetah?
He was trying to pull a fast one.

Did you read about the little boy who was taken to hospital at the weekend after swallowing a dozen coins from a vending machine?
Doctors are hoping the coins will pass through him, but as of yesterday there was still no change.

If people who are too addicted to nicotine have to get a nicotine patch, does someone who is addicted to eating cabbages have to get a cabbage patch?

My dog, Minton, swallowed a shuttlecock.
Bad Minton.

What do you call a dinosaur that uses cheap toilet paper?
Megasorass.

I was going to tell you a joke about a helicopter, but it would probably go over your head.

Don't feel too sorry for Humpty Dumpty.

He may have had a terrible summer but he had a great fall.

Why was the politician always out of breath?
He was running for office.

Did you read about the man who bent down to pick up a sieve and strained himself?

What did the female rook say to the other female rook when they met up at the end of the nesting season?
"Bred any good rooks lately?"

"DAD, I KNOW I'M GOING TO REGRET ASKING YOU THIS, BUT WHY DO YOU CALL THE LAPTOP PRINTER BOB MARLEY?"

"BECAUSE IT'S ALWAYS JAMMIN'"

I told my suitcases that they wouldn't be going away on holiday this year. So now I've had to deal with a lot of emotional baggage.

I told my daughter that I had made a fully operational car out of spaghetti.
She didn't believe me until I drove pasta.

Did you hear about the church janitor who was also the organist? He had to mind his keys and pews.

Why did the dog's owner think that his pet was a great mathematician?
Because when he asked the dog what five minus five was, the dog said nothing.

What was the name of that French boy at your school who never wore shoes?
Oh yes, I remember – Philippe Flop.

Did you see that advert in the paper?
It said: "Dead budgie for sale. Not going cheep."

Why did the housekeeper put her feet up and rest after she had finished doing the last of the ironing?
Because she had nothing pressing to attend to.

What did the sink say to the toilet?
You look a little flushed.

Did you read about the woman who passed out on the airport luggage carousel?
She slowly came around.

6.30 is the best time on a clock.
Hands down.

I left my wife because she was totally obsessed with counting.
I wonder what she's up to now.

"DAD, I'M HUNGRY."

"HI, HUNGRY. I'M DAD."

Air at petrol stations used to be free, but now they charge £1.20 to pump air into your tyres.
I guess that's inflation for you.

What did the grape say when somebody stepped on it?
Nothing, it just let out a little wine.

Did you read about the stand-up comedian who did a show for a cannibal tribe?
He went down really well.

Will glass coffins prove to be a success?
Remains to be seen.

What did Cinderella say when the camera film she had sent to the pharmacy had still not been developed?
"Someday my prints will come."

What's the best type of music to listen to when you're fishing?
Something catchy.

What was the name of that girl in your class who could juggle three bottles of Budweiser?
Oh yes, I remember – Beatrix.

Did you hear about the man who was nervous about taking part in a bug-eating contest?
Two days before and he already had butterflies in his stomach.

Why didn't the dentist enjoy going on a date with a manicurist?
Because they fought tooth and nail.

I used to go out with a woman who always carried a taser.
She was stunning.

"DAD MY NOSE IS RUNNING."

"WELL, YOU'D BETTER RUN AFTER IT."

What do you call a man with an elephant on his head?
An ambulance.

If you see two bugs crawling around among the crumbs on your dinner plate and you have to choose one to eat, which should you choose?
Always the lesser of two weevils.

Did you read about the man who is terrified of elevators?
He says he's taking steps to avoid them.

What was the name of that girl in your class who had a Saturday job in a beauty salon operating the sunbeds?
Oh yes, I remember – Tanya.

What's the difference between a cranky two-year-old and a duckling?
One is a whiny toddler and the other is a tiny waddler.

Why did the man deliberately drive his car into the lake one night?
So that he could dip his headlights.

Why are pirates called pirates?
They just ARRRR!

What does a painter do when he gets cold?
He puts on another coat.

Did you read about the man who was trying to phone a Tibetan spiritual leader but instead ended up ordering a four-legged pack animal?
He had mistakenly called Dial A Llama.

I once knew a girl who had trouble written all over her.
It wasn't the most artistic of tattoos.

"HEY, DAD, I WAS THINKING."

"I THOUGHT I COULD SMELL SOMETHING BURNING."

Did you hear about the man who drank a whole bottle of invisible ink?
He's at the hospital waiting to be seen.

Why did the pony ask for a glass of water?
Because it was a little horse.

I went on Amazon to buy a lighter, but all they had were 4,867 matches.

Why was the baby ant confused?
Because all his uncles were ants.

Did you hear about the pregnant bedbug?
She's going to have her baby in the spring.

Why aren't there any aspirins in the jungle?
Because the parrots eat 'em all.

What do you get if you cross a pit bull with a golden retriever?
A dog that will bite your leg off and then bring it back to you.

Did you hear about the magician who could only do half a trick?
He was a member of the Magic Semi-Circle.

Why did the coffee taste like dirt?
Because it was ground just a few minutes ago.

What did Frank Sinatra say when he was asked if he had ever kept wading birds as pets?
"Egrets, I've had a few..."

I wanted to discuss with my wife her unfortunate habit of always overcooking French fries, but it was a bit of a hot potato.

"HOW DID YOU SLEEP LAST NIGHT, DAD?"

"LIKE A LOG – I WOKE UP IN THE FIREPLACE."

Did you read that a truck carrying two tons of onions overturned on the motorway in Lancashire, blocking all three lanes?

Drivers are advised to find a hard shoulder to cry on.

I recently opened a deer cloning business.

It's for anyone wanting to make a quick buck.

What was the name of that boy in your class who always preferred not to stand?
Oh yes, I remember – Neil.

Where do surfers learn to surf?
At boarding school.

My wife is furious that the woman who lives next door has started sunbathing nude in her garden.
Personally, I'm on the fence.

If you see a crime take place at the Apple store, what does it make you?
An iWitness.

Did you read about the athlete who fired his masseuse?
She kept rubbing him up the wrong way.

When I moved into my new igloo, my friends threw me a surprise house-warming party.
So now I'm homeless.

Did you read about the man who sued an airline for misplacing all his luggage?
Unfortunately, he lost his case.

Why didn't the hippie save his daughter's toy when it was floating away in the sea?
Because it was pretty far out, man.

"I'M ABSOLUTELY STARVING, DAD. I FEEL LIKE A GIANT TUB OF ICE CREAM."

"THAT'S FUNNY. YOU DON'T LOOK LIKE ONE."

I have to admit that waking up this morning was an eye-opening experience.

What was the name of that girl in your class who set fire to all of her father's statements from a loan company?
Oh yes, I remember – Bernadette.

Did you read about the man who drove his expensive car into a tree and found out how his Mercedes bends?

Why are people who carry bees considered good-looking?
Because beauty is in the eye of the bee-holder.

Do you want to hear a joke about time travel?
Actually it doesn't matter – you didn't like it.

I once had a door-to-door fruit delivery business, but it didn't last because I drove people bananas.

Did you see that a Vicks VapoRub truck spilled its entire load after overturning on the highway this morning?
Incredibly, there was no congestion for eight hours.

You know a job I could really see myself doing?
Inspecting mirrors.

Did you read about the serious accident at the army base?
A jeep ran over a bag of popcorn and killed four kernels.

How do you stop a dog from smelling?
Put a clothes peg on its nose.

"DAD, WILL YOU TAKE THE BIN BAG OUT TONIGHT?"

"SURE. WHERE DO YOU RECKON? A NICE ROMANTIC MEAL OR A MOVIE?"

My four-year-old daughter has been taking Spanish lessons for over a year and yet she still can't say "please" in Spanish.
I think that's poor for four.

Did you read about the two circus acrobats who got married?
They say they're heels over head in love.

My wife complained that her feet hurt. I said, "I'm not surprised. You've got your shoes on the wrong feet."
She said, "But these are the only feet I've got."

I once went to a fancy-dress party as a turtle.
I walked in with a girl on my back and whenever anyone asked who she was I said, "That's Michelle."

Did you read that some aquatic mammals escaped from their enclosure at the zoo yesterday?
For three hours it was otter chaos.

What was the name of that girl in your class who always used to play the mouth organ?
It will come to me in a minute... Hah! Monica!

"DAD, WHAT BOOK ARE YOU READING NOW?"

"IT'S A HORROR STORY IN BRAILLE. SOMETHING BAD IS GOING TO HAPPEN, I CAN FEEL IT."

The other day, I bet the butcher that he couldn't reach the meat that was on the top shelf.
He refused, saying the steaks were too high.

Why did town planners reject the architect's proposal for a 295-storey tower block?
They said his design had too many flaws.

Did you hear about the man who was convinced that moose were falling from the sky?
Until his wife explained to him: "It's only reindeer."

What did one plate say to the other plate?
"Tonight, dinner's on me."

Did you read the story about the bumper-car operator who got fired from his job?
He says he's suing his employer for funfair dismissal.

I'm very proud of the Victorian hatchet I own that was once used for chopping citrus trees and I love to tell stories about it.
But my wife thinks it's boring and says it's just an antique lime axe.

"DAD, DO YOU KNOW THERE'S A HOLE IN MY T-SHIRT?"

"NO. WHO SINGS IT?"

What was the name of that boy in your class who would never accept that any of his tennis shots were out?
Oh yes, I remember – Justin.

Why do you never see elephants hiding in trees?
Because they're so good at it.

What's the difference between an egg, a rug and a nice lie-in on a Sunday morning?
You can beat an egg, you can beat a rug, but you can't beat a nice lie-in on a Sunday morning.

Did you hear that there was chaos and confusion in town today when the stationery store moved?

In history class have you studied the 19th-century French general who was killed after stepping on a land mine? I forget his name. No, wait, it's come to me.

Napoleon Blown Apart.

What's the difference between a hippo and a zippo?
One is really heavy and the other is a little lighter.

Did you read about the woman who was a compulsive collector of magazines?
Apparently she had a lot of issues.

"DAD, I'M STRUGGLING WITH MY MATHS HOMEWORK. IF I HAD NINE APPLES AND ATE FIVE, WHAT WOULD I GET?"

"INDIGESTION."

To the person who stole my case of energy drinks, I hope you can't sleep at night.

Did you hear about the man who left his fortune to California's San Andreas National Wildlife Refuge?
He was generous to a fault.

What was the name of that boy in your class who often had cat scratches all the way up his arms?
Oh yes, I remember – Claude.

I took my wife to an orchard and we stared at the trees for over an hour.
I later learned that this was not the Apple watch she had been expecting for her birthday.

Did you read about the diminutive psychic who is on the run from the police?
Yes, a small medium is at large.

Why did the scarecrow win an award?
Because he was outstanding in his field.

Did you see that yesterday in the Pacific Ocean a ship carrying a cargo of red paint collided with a ship carrying a cargo of purple paint?
Both crews were marooned.

Why were Sherlock Holmes's tax bills always so low?
Because he was a master of deduction.

I once had a vivid nightmare that I was in Panama during a snowstorm.
I must have been dreaming of a white isthmus.

"DAD, WHAT'S ON THE TV?"

"DUST, MOSTLY."

What does Batman say to Robin before they get in the Batmobile?
"Robin, get in the Batmobile."

Did you read about the butcher who accidentally backed into his meat slicer and got a little behind in his work?

What's the difference between a jeweller and a jailer?
A jeweller sells watches and a jailer watches cells.

Why did the nuts and olives in bowls on the hotel bar say nice things about all the customers?
They were the complimentary snacks.

Two flies landed on the sweet fruit of a tropical palm tree.
Both later agreed it was the best date they had ever been on.

Did you read about the man who barged into the doctor's because he was convinced that he was a snooker ball?
The doctor told him to get to the end of the cue.

What was the name of that girl in your class who was always pushing and elbowing people out of the way?
Oh yes, I remember – Jocelyn.

"DAD, I PASSED MR MONTAGUE OUTSIDE THE SUPERMARKET."

"THAT MUST HAVE BEEN PAINFUL."

I once bought a caterpillar cake without checking the "best before" date.
So I ended up with a butterfly cake.

How does Darth Vader like his toast?
On the dark side.

Did you read about the man who lost his left arm and his left leg in an accident?
He's all right now.

What did the vicar say at the salad bar?
"Lettuce pray."

What did one elevator say to the other elevator?
"I think I'm coming down with something."

Did you hear about the wedding of the two florists?
It was an arranged marriage.

What do you get when you play tug-of-war with a pig?
Pulled pork.

Why are fish so easy to weigh?
Because they have their own set of scales.

Did you hear about the optician's patient who became annoyed whenever he said A, E, I, O or U when reading the eye-test chart?
The optician said that as well as needing new glasses, the patient had irritable vowel syndrome.

I was wrongly stopped for speeding 144 times last year. I've now written to the police to complain about this gross injustice.

Did you read about the Dutch girl who wore inflatable shoes?
Sadly, she popped her clogs.

Why was the vulture thrown off the plane?
Because the other passengers complained about his carrion luggage.

"DAD, CAN YOU CLEAR THE TABLE?"

"I'LL TRY, BUT I MIGHT NEED A LONG RUN-UP."

What was the name of that boy in your class who liked exploring rabbit holes?
Oh yes, I remember – Warren.

What's the best way to communicate with fish?
Drop them a line.

Did you hear about the man who dreamed every night for a week that he wrote *The Lord of the Rings*?
He was Tolkien in his sleep.

Why does E.T. have such big eyes?
Because he saw his phone bill.

What's E.T. short for?
Because he's only got little legs.

Did you hear that the council finance officer who has racked up such huge debts is now in hospital with severe constipation?
He can't budget.

Have you read the sad story about the woman who was fired from her job in a calendar factory?
All she did was take a day off.

"DAD, WILL YOU BE ABLE TO PICK ME UP LATER?"

"IT DEPENDS HOW HEAVY YOU ARE."

Do you know what award they gave to the person who invented the door knocker?
The no-bell prize.

My cardiologist friend keeps sending me X-rays of his chest.
It's a bit weird, I know, but at least it shows his heart is in the right place.

Why are soldiers always tired on 1 April?
Because they've just had a 31-day March.

What do you call a fly without wings?
A walk.

Did you read about the two slices of bread that got married?
Everything was lovely until one of the guests decided to toast the bride and groom.

What was the name of that girl in your class who was quite round and had yellow skin?
Oh yes, I remember – Melanie.

Why did the thief take a long shower before robbing the bank?
He wanted to make a clean getaway.

"DAD, HOW LONG WILL DINNER BE?"

"FOUR INCHES. WE'RE HAVING SAUSAGES."

Did you read that the world tongue-twister champion has been arrested?
I reckon they're going to give him a really tough sentence.

Did you see that rock band the Teddy Bears have had to cancel tonight's gig because all their plectrums had been stolen?
Yes, today's the day the Teddy Bears had their picks nicked.

What was the name of that girl in your class who went out to dinner with Henry, and what happened to her?
Oh yes, I remember – Henrietta.